NLP for Parents

Judy Bartkowiak

First edition published in 2010

© Copyright 2010

Judy Bartkowiak

Paperback ISBN 978-1-907685-46-0

ePub ISBN 978-1-907685-47-7

Mobipocket/Kindle ISBN 978-1-907685-48-4

Published in the UK by MX Publishing

335 Princess Park Manor, Royal Drive, London, N11 3GX

www.mxpublishing.co.uk

Cover design by

www.staunch.com

ABOUT THE AUTHOR

Judy Bartkowiak is an NLP (Neuro Linguistic Programming) Master Practitioner with specialised training in working with children. She is also a qualified Personal and Pastoral Counsellor.

She is passionate about introducing NLP to kids both directly or by teaching it to parents. She runs a therapy practice working with parents, teachers, children and teens. Although she is based in the UK she also offers consultation across the world via Skype and telephone.

She says, "Having four children myself I have observed a wide range of parenting styles and talked with hundreds of mums and dads. This workbook covers what I feel are the most useful aspects of NLP for parents. I feel they are life changing concepts.

I am really passionate about NLP for kids. Ever since I was first introduced to NLP by Sue Knight, (author of NLP at Work and an NLP Trainer), I have been guided by NLP principles as a parent and found them to bring about truly remarkable results."

Before her four children started school, Judy ran a Montessori Nursery School for 7 years and became aware of just how differently children learn and communicate.

Judy then returned to her career as a Market Research Consultant and used her understanding and enjoyment of working with children to specialise in children's products and TV shows.

She ran hundreds of focus groups over the next 15 years with parents and children of all ages advising companies on what kids like.

She qualified in Neuro Linguistic Programming in 2001-2004 and made a career change which led Judy to taking Open University qualifications in Creative Writing. She then embarked on a writing career which has included writing children's books, copywriting and writing NLP books.

If you'd like to ask Judy about your parenting issue, be trained in NLP or arrange a coaching session for your child or teenager, email her at judy@engagingnlp.com.

ENGAGING NLP

Neuro Linguistic Programming is a way of life,
a new and different, positive approach to the
way we communicate and how we interpret the
way others communicate with us both verbally
and non-verbally.

The only way to make effective changes in our
life is to engage with this new way and
incorporate it daily into everything we do.

At home, at work or at play, whether we are a
child, a teenager or an adult, we can make new
choices about how we live our life so that we
achieve all we wish for in our friendships,
relationships and our own state of well-being
and happiness.

Engage with NLP and see, hear and feel the
difference immediately.

CONTENTS

Page

INTRODUCTION

NLP is a completely different way of viewing your world. Once you have been introduced to the NLP way of thinking and communicating it will seem like you've come home. It is respectful of others and more importantly of yourself and it is positive.

John Grinder and Richard Bandler developed what they came to call NLP from a combination of Virginia Satir's Family Therapy, Franz Perls' Gestalt Therapy and the work of Milton Erickson in the area of language patterns.

What Grinder and Bandler added was the idea of coding excellence. They studied how successful and effective people communicated and formulated some ground rules that would bring these results to anyone who applied them. These ground rules are what we call NLP or Neuro Linguistic Programming.

This book is designed first and foremost to be a practical workbook for you to use, write in and apply on a day to day basis.

If you'd like to read about this subject in more depth, I have written a book in the Teach Yourself series entitled 'Be a happier parent with NLP' published by Hodder Education, which provides plenty of detail, case studies and examples.

NLP workbooks available in the *Engaging NLP* series are:

NLP for Children

NLP for Teens

NLP for Parents

NLP for Teachers

NLP Back to Work

NLP Sport

NLP Exercise and Fitness

NLP Pregnancy and Birth

NLP Setting up your own business

NLP Getting a job

THE GROUND RULES

NLP has a number of ground rules or principles that form the basis for all the practical tools and techniques you will learn in this book.

I find that they underpin it in such a way that if I get stuck, just by applying one of these rules I can find a solution.

Each one makes you stop and think differently. It challenges you to assess whether what you do now, works or if by changing it, you could get a better outcome.

NLP is completely focussed on positivity, aiming for a positive outcome, a compelling outcome that is desirable for you. The focus is on what you want, rather than what you don't want.

There are even some toxic words that by avoiding will steer you a positive, resourceful path.

NLP uses a great deal too much jargon in my opinion and so I have reworded some of the concepts to make them more digestible as you will want to pass them on to your children.

1) If you always do what you've always done

then you will always get what you've always got

This is a great one to start with because it really challenges you to change.

What it says is that if the result you are getting such as your children's behaviour is not what you want then you must change your own behaviour in order to get a different result.

We tend to think as parents that it is their behaviour that must be changed and we carry on telling them off, shouting at them and getting cross.

So here is a new way of thinking.

Do something different.

If you do something different you will get a different result.

The first way to do this is to decide what result you want. There could be any number of results such as children doing what they are told, not throwing things, shouting and so on.

Think of a situation that occurs frequently in your family that you'd like to change. Write it down here.

I want to change………..

Now think about what you would like to happen. What is your desirable outcome? Write that down now.

What I want to happen is.........

When you decide on what result you want you need to be quite specific and get to the detail. What exactly do you want, from whom, when and in what way? Write this down here.

I want ....

The more specific you can be about what you want to happen the easier it will be to decide how to change what you are currently doing in order to achieve it.

Your current behaviour pattern is dictated by your beliefs. The reason you are shouting or using the words you are using, telling them to do certain things is because you have a belief that it is important for them to do what you ask.

This belief stems from your own childhood and how you were brought up, what you consider to be of value and important about how to bring up children. This may also have come from the mores of the culture you are from, the area or region and who you spend time with in your environment.

If what you are doing is not working then look at the underlying belief for this behaviour.

Are you sure your underlying belief is sound? Could you be carrying forward into the present a belief that belongs in the past?

Look back at the situation you have written about and list all the beliefs that underpin your thinking. What do you hold in your head about what should happen in that situation?

I believe that............

I believe that.............

I believe that..............

Where have those beliefs come from?

Are they valid for you today? Are they serving you well or making life more difficult?

Could you re-think a belief so that you could make other choices of behaviour?

Whenever you find yourself thinking 'I should do....' - change it to, 'I could do...' so that you give yourself permission to do something different.

Do your beliefs limit your choices of behaviour? Increase your options and change your behaviour to get the result you want.

This is of course an excellent challenge for children. How often do they repeat the same behaviour, get the same result and wish they'd got another one. They have the same choices as you.

Ask them what they want to happen in the situation and ask them to describe it in detail, even act it out if that helps.

Then ask them what they could do differently to make this result happen for them.

Discuss with them their different options and how likely each one would bring about the outcome they desire.

This process requires that they step into the shoes of the other people involved in the situation rather than just look at it from their point of view. This is an enormously powerful tool that they can learn as a toddler and apply throughout their life.

2) *You have the resources to do whatever you want to do*

You have a huge resource of skills that you have been building since childhood. Each one, when applied in different contexts gives you yet more skills and options.

Lots of parents think that they have no skills but that is not so. In the hurly burly of parenthood it's easy to feel overwhelmed and feel we can't cope.

So if you are feeling a low sense of self belief like that, imagine that someone else is watching you over the course of the day. What would they observe? What would they see you do?

What you do automatically or unconsciously is a skill that someone else would observe and admire. Pretend you are someone who doesn't know you, observing all you do.

- Look at each thing you do over the course of the day and write down the skill you use to do that thing. Make a list here.

- What do you believe about doing this thing? How important is the way you do it? How well do you feel you do this thing?

The reason I do……………………………

well is because I believe…….

The reason I do……………………………

well is because I believe…….

The reason I do...............................

well is because I believe.......

The reason I do...............................

well is because I believe.......

Now list each thing you do well and give each
one a score out of 10 for how important it is to
you to do this thing well.

1.

2.

3.

4.

5.

6.

7.

8.

- Now look at each thing you do and ask yourself, 'What does that also mean I can do?'

  Write that down in a list here. You may be surprised at how you can use a skill in many different parts of your life.

- Whenever you are struggling

    o identify the skill you need

    o think about when and where you had that skill

    o ask yourself, what was the belief you had that enabled you to use that skill

    o take on that belief now in order to access the skill.

When we talk about taking on a belief in NLP we mean that we change our belief. A belief is not a value. A value is a code you live by and that is not likely to change as it is instilled in you as a child and is governed by both your upbringing and your environment.

A belief is something you hold about the things you do and changes as you experience new situations and people. For example, you certainly hold different beliefs now from those you held as a child such as believing in Father Christmas or the Tooth Fairy!

Our beliefs about parenthood will have changed as a result of becoming a parent and continue to change as they do.

3) *If someone else can do it you can too*

This is a very empowering belief to take on board as a parent, isn't it? How often do we see other parents do things that we admire and would like to do ourselves?

If you have noticed a skill in someone else, the chances are that in some way you too have this skill because that is how you come to have noticed it in the first place. We say 'if you spot it, you've got it!'

You can acquire these new skills and hone existing ones by modelling (or copying) it in someone who demonstrates that skill with excellence.

How do we do it?

a) First we need to identify the skill we want.

We do this by observation. Observe and be intently curious about what you see and how your model (the person you want the skill from) behaves.

Watch every part of the skill, the non-verbal cues such as body language and the verbal ones, the tone of voice, language patterns, volume and pace.

Identify which part of the skill you need because it is unlikely you need all of it.

Decide which bit you need and break it into small parts that you can practice.

b) Think about the belief your model would have in order to use that skill.

Do this by reflecting 'If I did that I would be thinking I was ....'. Perhaps your model sounds confident or calm, controlled or firm?

Where in your life do you have that belief? Maybe you have that belief when you are at work, with your friends or at the gym?

Think hard about where you have the belief and visualise yourself in that situation where the belief is strong.

It's not unusual for parents to have skills at work that they leave at work!

Even if you are a 'stay at home' mum or dad or are doing a different job now you have children, those skills are still part of your repertoire and may need to be brought into your parenting role. So dust off that skill and belief so that you have them now in your parenting role.

When you use NLP with your children it is very useful to be able to show them where they have skills that you observe at home, so that they can take them into school along with the underlying belief about having the skill.

  c) Now practice the precise skill you have
      identified.   You can do this on your own
      first and then practice on the family.

Notice what results you get and keep practising until you get your desirable outcome.

You may find that you need more models of that skill so you can observe different executions of it and talk to the models about how they do it and what they believe about the way they do it. It often takes a few different models of a skill to help you acquire it for yourself and use in a way that works for you.

26

Once you have mastered this modelling exercise you can show your children how to do it.

Remember that you are a natural model for your children because they are observing you every day and will unconsciously be modelling you and those you interact with regularly.

If your children are doing something you don't like; you may need to check that you aren't unconsciously modelling this behaviour yourself. It may not be an exact copy but ask yourself, is there any part of my life when I am like this?

How often do we hear a child sounding just like one of their parents? We laugh when they come out with an expression or mannerism we have, so you need to model the behaviour you want from them rather than what you don't want.

You may need to demonstrate a skill quite deliberately to make a point even saying, 'watch how mummy does this'.

If you are having food issues with your children not eating what you've cooked; then eat with them because you eating the same meal will encourage them to copy you.

Involve your partner because they are important role models, especially for boys. Teachers will often observe how boys who are poor readers have dads who don't read in their child's presence.

Use modelling skills as part of your ongoing personal development and show your children how to follow your lead.

4) There is no failure only feedback

As parents we often feel we have failed don't we? Things don't always go as we'd like and when that happens we get upset and feel we've failed as parents.

However, imagine you held a belief that there is no failure only feedback, how much more reassuring is that?

What NLP says is that you cannot 'not communicate'. Whether that is verbal or non verbal communication, simply by your existence you are communicating something.

For example, if we look across the road and see a teenager, we notice their clothes, hair, body language and maybe hear what they are saying.

We haven't personally had any interaction with them but already they have communicated to us and we have a response.

The response we feel and the response we get from others is a result of our communication in the same way. So we are communicating all the time and receiving communication back.

The communication we receive is feedback. The feedback can be verbal or non verbal and we can use it to learn more about what and how we are communicating.

It is not failure; in the same way as the teenager mentioned earlier has not failed in any way. He or she has elicited a response in us that reflects our own beliefs and values.

How we choose to respond will be determined by these and other people will respond and give feedback depending on their own beliefs and values.

There is no <u>one</u> correct or definitive response.

When someone responds negatively to you, including your children, remember that they are giving you feedback that you can choose to accept or not, depending on whether it seems reasonable when set against your beliefs and values.

Their feedback is not a fact of life but simply their opinion at that moment and this will be influenced by their own internal state or mood and yours, of course.

You may be getting negative feedback because someone is just in a bad mood, feeling rough, depressed, or cross about something unrelated that has happened to them.

You have two choices when you get negative feedback. You can choose to accept it or reject it.

Accept it if you think they may have a fair point and take the opportunity to reword what you said or do something differently. By doing this you are using the feedback as an adult learning experience that will enable you to communicate in rapport next time.

Children often give very clear negative feedback and we are hurt and angry. They do this because we are safe targets. They know we love them and will be hurt by what they say. It's possible that they do this most when they are hurting and feeling insecure themselves.

However difficult it might be at the time, if you believe they are being reasonable in their feedback, thank them for the feedback and do something different. This might mean saying something in a different way or doing something in a different way.

By doing this you are modelling for them how you would like them to respond to the negative feedback they will undoubtedly get through life, from school, work and socially.

If however, when you reflect on what they said or their non verbal feedback, you decide that it is unreasonable then you can choose to ignore it or say that you don't agree with the negative feedback.

Instead of feeling you have failed when you get negative feedback, reframe this with its positive intention which is for you to learn from it.

We can learn more from feedback and help our children learn from it if we avoid the following types of comment:

a) Generalisations

These are when we tell our children that they 'always' leave the door open or 'never' tidy their room, 'everyone' works harder than them or 'no-one' goes out weekday evenings.

Generalisations are rarely true so they aren't useful to learn from. In fact it's when you think of the exceptions that you learn anything revealing and it's worth pointing that out instead. For example, 'thank you for closing the door, when you did that I was really pleased'. Focus on the behaviour you do want, not what you don't want.

b) Deletions

When we delete the context of feedback it isn't very helpful. Saying 'that's better' or 'work harder', 'play nicely' isn't specific and needs some detail so children know when they've got it right. 'Take it in turns to play with the red car' is more specific so children know what's expected of them.

c) Distortions

Sometimes we make assumptions about what our children are doing and why they are doing it and this is not helpful as we can't know this. We are not mind readers so we are in effect distorting the facts.

We might say, 'you're deliberately annoying me' or 'you're making me cross'. They aren't. What is really happening is that we are choosing to be cross or annoyed so we should tell them this instead and focus on the behaviour.

5) *If you try, you won't succeed*

How many times a day do we assure people that we will 'try' and do something? Why do we use that word 'try'?

It's because we know deep down that we may not actually have the time or inclination to do it.

Perhaps we think we don't have the skill? We want to hedge our bets really, don't we? We don't want to give a promise that we may not be able to keep and we don't want to let people down.

We also don't want to say 'no' possibly because that would appear confrontational or provoke further discussion which we don't have the time or desire to pursue. So off we go to 'try' and do that thing, knowing that we don't have to do it, we just have to 'try' to do it.

What does 'trying to do it' look like? Well it looks like someone accepting that they can't and won't do it fairly shortly after they've said they'll 'try'.

So when we ask children to 'try' to do something we can expect the same response, can't we?

We remember perhaps our own parents urging us to 'just try your best'. Yet there is built-in failure in the word 'try'.

Notice when you use this word and reword your sentence without the word 'try' so children will be more motivated. 'Try' presupposes they will find it difficult so they are expecting to give up on the exercise more quickly than if your expectation was that they could do it.

Imagine there are two boxes in front of you and I ask you to pick up the first one. You will pick it up quite easily because you assume it must be light.

Now I ask you to 'try' and pick up the other. Immediately you expect the other box to be heavier and you may have difficulty picking it up. If I then said, 'try hard' or 'just try it', I am emphasising the difficulty and you may look at it wondering how heavy it is and even consider asking for help.

In fact the boxes are the same weight. The only difference is our expectations of how heavy the second box is.

Sometimes you might be asking your children to do something that you believe to be genuinely hard. However, they may not find it as hard as you expect. Express it as something they <u>can</u> do rather than something they can't do.

There is built-in failure in the word 'try'.

Just 'do it'.

6) *The map is not the territory*

What this means is that how you see the world is different from how others see it. We all have different perceptions of our environment depending on our age, life stage, culture and experiences. To assume our perceptions are the only correct ones would be unecological in NLP terms.

This is ever obvious when you consider how your children see their world. Their map is very different from ours.

Their priorities are different and based on a very small map mostly involving them! They have no or very little awareness of the bigger picture that we see and as parents we usually want to protect them from this for a while at least.

Children inhabit a quite insular space centred on the home and school plus a small area of community. It is a world where they feel safe and loved, where the worst thing they can think of is that world changing.

Children fear change because so much is still unknown to them and they have no experience of it to reassure them that they will be OK.

When we encounter change we usually have something similar that we can draw on for reassurance and confidence. We can help children cope with change in the same way.

If our children need to make a change we can remind them of how well they have coped with changes they have experienced such as the birth of a sibling, moving to a new room, going on holiday and making friends, starting at nursery school and so on.

When you need to understand your children's map, instead of drawing on your own experiences of being a child (although that can help) ask them about it.

We can use metaphors to help children express their feelings. Whilst asking a direct 'how do you feel about that?' question to an adult works reasonably well, it doesn't with children.

Ask children instead to equate it to something they are familiar with by asking them 'what is joining a new class like?' or 'who are you when you have to answer a question in class?'

Children will happily draw on characters they know on TV or video games, friends they know, animals or may even be able to equate it to another experience they have had.

To find out more, simply reflect back what they have said in question form. We call this using a 'clean' question.

So if your child has said that starting a new class is like being a small animal in a large scary jungle, you can say 'a small animal in a large scary jungle?'

Enter their territory by stepping into their shoes and seeing it from their viewpoint.

7) *Look for the pay off*

Sometimes as parents we find ourselves doing things we don't want to do and may even feel resentful about. This could be something as major as a career change or work choice or it could be relatively minor such as changing nappies.

Whatever we do though, we can look for the positive intention by reframing it or looking at it from another angle. Be creative and find some good things about what you don't like doing.

This is a great skill to teach children because they have less control over their environment than we do; so being able to put a positive gloss on unpleasant things will really help them through life.

The other way to use this skill is to reframe and look for the pay off in your children's behaviour. When they are not doing what you've asked; consider what they are getting out of this behaviour. They may want your attention or they may know from experience that this behaviour will lead to you giving in and letting them have their own way. They may be expecting a bribe from you such as 'if you stop this now, I'll take you to McDonalds later'. If you make it worth their while to play up, then this is their positive intention or pay off.

We can use this knowledge to encourage good behaviour by giving them a pay-off for the good behaviour we want rather than the bad behaviour. We do things for a reason. If we see behaviour we don't want, consider other ways to give the pay off without getting the behaviour.

This next section covers some very hands on NLP tools and techniques to learn and add to your parenting skills.

1. Rapport

2. Logical levels for change

3. Anchoring

4. Time Lines

5. Conflict

1: RAPPORT

<u>What is it?</u>

You know what rapport is with your friends because you naturally use similar expressions, words, body language and tone of voice. You were attracted to each other by your similarities so you probably don't need to work hard at communicating.

What about rapport with your child though? Do you both speak the same language? How would you know?

There are 3 languages, visual, auditory and kinaesthetic.

Visual

You think in pictures and images, using expressions like 'do you see what I mean' or 'look at it from my point of view'.

Your descriptions will have colour and texture and views and your surroundings will be important to you as will your appearance. If you are visual, how your baby or child looks will be important as will their room. If your surroundings don't look nice this may upset you more than most.

If your child is visual expect them to make a fuss over what they wear, how their hair looks and the colour of whatever you are buying for them. They will enjoy art and looking at the pictures in books and they may be early readers. They will not necessarily notice what you say to them though!

Auditory

You are auditory if you enjoy music, notice the sounds around you and prefer your friends to call rather than text or email. You tend to remember what people say to you or what you've heard on the radio better than what you've read.

You will find the sound of a baby crying or children shouting more disturbing than other mums. You might use expressions like 'did you hear what I said?' or 'please be quiet'.

An auditory child usually makes a lot of noise and sounds are important to them. They will like singing, musical instruments and toys that have sounds.

They learn to read best by hearing the phonetic sounds of the words and learn numbers with CDs or songs.

Kinaesthetic

You are an active person and enjoy being on the go. Exercise and fitness is important to you and you like to have physical contact with your friends and your family.

You notice the temperature and feel uncomfortable if it's not right.

You may use expressions like 'let's get going' or 'that doesn't feel right' because you are very sensitive to atmosphere.

A kinaesthetic child wants cuddles and action. Sitting still isn't easy and they need to have things to do.

They need to be shown what to do rather than told and they like to be helping you and getting involved in what's going on. They will enjoy construction toys and role playing, dressing up and playing video games that are interactive.

How do we use this?

Once you know what you are and what your child is you can easily match their preference. You both will use all three but there will be one dominant one that probably won't change even as they grow up.

You match by using the same words and expressions as your child so they understand you. It's as easy as that!

You can achieve even better rapport by getting onto their level and matching their body language, facial expressions and their tone of voice. It may seem strange at first but they don't notice when you match if you do it well.

You can match even with a baby as they mimic you quite naturally. You can use this to take the lead and get them to sleep! Match them for a while to establish rapport and then start making your own actions for them to copy such as pretending to go to sleep.

Barriers to rapport

Rapport breaks down when you use what we can deletions, distortions and generalisations because they are confusing to a child.

Deletions are when you give vague instructions such as 'tidy up your room' or 'be good' without providing detailed context.

Distortions are when you say what you imagine them to be thinking or what you think will happen in the future such as 'You are going to fall' or 'I know what you're up to'.

It's better to comment on what you observe and check out with them, so 'are you OK or shall I hold your hand' and 'are you playing with my phone?' are much clearer communications for children.

Generalisations are when you use words like 'always' and 'never' and 'everyone'. Focus on what they are doing now without reference to a pattern that you are exaggerating for effect. Notice when they get things right.

The word 'don't' is what NLP calls an embedded command. If you say to a child, 'Don't climb on there you will fall off!' Immediately they imagine themselves falling off and will be more likely to do just that. The example usually given is 'Don't think about pink elephants'. You have to imagine a pink elephant first in order not to do it.

Children respond best when they are told what to do not what 'not to do'. Focus on what you do want.

Rapport is about communicating and you cannot 'not communicate' because we do it all the time both verbally and non-verbally with our children.

2: LOGICAL LEVELS FOR CHANGE

What is it

When we are thinking about making a change in our lives we need to be aware of the level of the change we want to make and what levels below it will need to be changed first. For example if we want to change our behaviour we need to consider what we have to do about our environment to facilitate the change in behaviour.

Say we are thinking of getting a new job (a behaviour change) unless we organise childcare, have the support of our partner and have the qualifications and experience needed for the job (environment) then it won't happen.

If the change you want to make is higher up at the skills level or even identity, you can see that each level below the one you're changing will also need to be changed because each one underpins the one above.

If you're feeling overwhelmed or want to make changes in your life it helps to work your way up from the bottom looking at each level.

Start with your environment and think about where you live, work and the cultures of those places. How does your environment affect you? What could you change about it that would make a difference?

Once you've done worksheet 1 on rapport you will know whether you are visual, auditory or kinaesthetic. This may prompt you to make some changes in line with your preference.

What do you do? What are your patterns of behaviour? If you always do what you've always done you will always get what you've always got. If you are not happy with the outcomes, change your behaviour because you can't control other people's behaviour, not even your child's.

What are your skills? What are you good at? What did you used to be good at? Use the worksheet on time lines to revisit them and bring them to the present. A skill can be anything from being able to put on lipstick without a mirror or doing a cartwheel to being able to manage a meeting. The exercises you did in the Ground Rules section will help you here.

What beliefs do you hold about being a parent? Have you inherited beliefs from your own parents that are not working for you? Do they limit you? If that is so, use the time line to revisit these beliefs and decide whether you can replace them with a belief that will serve you better. We can change our beliefs and in fact we need to if we want to change our behaviour.

The values you hold will not change. These are the values you were brought up with and will pass on to your own children. Many of them will be part of your culture or environment. What values do you hold about being a parent? If you aren't living according to your values you will have a sense of disharmony. To correct this you will need to make changes to your beliefs, behaviour or environment because each level underpins the next.

Your identity is who you are, not the role you play at home and at work but the essential you. Who are you?

Exercise

A good way to think about this is to write down how other people would describe you. Write a list below.

My friends would describe me as

....

....

....

Imagine you are one of your friends or colleagues and 'disassociate', see yourself as others see you. We tend to be very self critical and judge ourselves severely, seeing the best in others rather than in ourselves.

This is a good time to do another exercise.

Exercise

Imagine a circle drawn on the floor or if you prefer use a mat or a piece of string.

This is your circle of excellence.

Step into it and think of all these great things your friends would say about you, think of things you have done that you are proud of and really associate into the good images, sounds and feelings that you experience in the circle.

Use the anchoring worksheet here to anchor this and you can use it whenever you need it.

Your purpose is at the top of the logical levels and refers to why we are here which is a big question. It may be one that has changed for you since becoming a parent and it affects all the logical levels so if you feel your purpose has changed, how does that affect your identity, values and beliefs, skills, behaviour and environment?

Parenthood is a time of change and it affects us in so many ways. It is important to take time to work through the levels and put them into harmony one with another.

3: ANCHORING

<u>When do we use it ?</u>

The metaphor of an anchor is very appropriate because when we feel adrift, lost, confused and overwhelmed by parenting it is helpful to put down an anchor to stabilize ourselves and find a calm place in my mind and body. We can rely on the anchor because it is heavy and solid and it won't let us down.

From there we can access our resources to move forward in what we're doing. We use anchoring to achieve a sense of control and resourcefulness in any situation.

Another reason to anchor is that sometimes we need to remind ourselves of good times to help us through more challenging times.

You can use it when

- The baby's crying and you've done everything (changed nappy, fed her, cuddled her etc). You want to cry too.

- School holidays and the kids are screaming at each other they are bored and you're clean out of ideas.

- Your toddler's has just refused to eat his food again and you've cooked it just the way he likes it.

- Your boss wants you to do a presentation but it's on your son's sports day and you feel torn

By 'resources' we mean the skills and strengths that you have acquired over the years. They can come from your childhood, from your youth, the workplace, travelling, anywhere.

The sense of calm you get from anchoring can help you find that inner resource and bring it out when and where you need it. You can anchor anywhere at any time and it takes seconds.

<u>What is it?</u>

Your anchor could be an image or a picture (if you are visual), a sound or piece of music (if you are auditory) or an action (if you are kinaesthetic). Use Worksheet 1 to decide which you are.

Choose an anchor that you can easily access anywhere because you need it to be something that doesn't draw attention to yourself in a social situation. If you are in a playground or park, a friend's house or a birthday party you probably won't want to be doing anything strange that people will notice.

Good anchors are natural actions such as picturing a scene or a painting if you are visual, quietly humming some bars of music if you are auditory or squeezing your ear lobe if you are kinaesthetic.

People in business and on the sports field use anchors when they want to access a particular strength; confidence, calm, energy, focus. You can have different anchors for different strengths.

You may already have some unconscious anchors. Some may work well for you such as the sight of you baby sleeping with a smile on her face may trigger a sense of pride that you're a good mum.

But does hearing the baby crying have the opposite effect?

Use a conscious anchor to over-ride the unconscious one.

<u>Step 1 – Establishing the anchor</u>

Close your eyes and think about when and where you feel calm and relaxed, strong and in control. Picture yourself there in that situation.

What can you see? Give the scene colour and clarity. Turn up the brightness and focus on everything in your picture.

What can you hear? Is there music, are people talking?

What are you doing? What is happening? Is it hot or cold, how do you feel?

When you really feel associated into the situation and as calm and confident as you could possibly be, fire the anchor. Do the thing you have decided to do as your anchor.

Step 2 – Break state

Think of something else for a moment just to relieve the tension. If you are visual, look at something else. If you are auditory hum a tune and if you are kinaesthetic, walk about for a minute.

Step 3 – Fire it again

Repeat step 1 and again make the images, sounds and feelings very strong before you fire the anchor.

Step 4 – Break state

Change your state for a minute – shake yourself or move about a bit.

Step 5 – Fire it again

Repeat the process. It will probably be quite quick by now.

Now you have your anchor, use it whenever you need that resource. You can establish different anchors for other resources.

Show your child how to do this as well. Even very small children can quickly anchor a feeling of being brave. You will need to help them recall when they were brave and describe it to them as they establish the anchor. Use the same words each time as this helps them remember it for themselves.

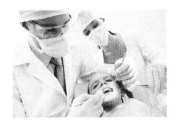

4: TIME LINE

What is it?

It is an imaginary line along the floor that represents time from at one end, the past through to the future at the other end. We usually start from a fairly central point to represent the present.

When do we use it?

When you've done it once you'll find all sorts of occasions to use a time line.

They're great for getting things into perspective when you feel a bit lost and lacking direction. If you've lost sight of your compelling vision you can walk back along the time line and find it to re-energise your goals.

If you find yourself saying 'I can't do...' use the time line to find out where that limiting belief came from.

When you experience grief or loss, whether that be for a person or a part of your life, you can travel back along the time line, find it and bring the parts you need now into the present.

You can use it with children who are having trouble adjusting to a change such as a new sibling or a house move. Step gently along the time line with them into the future and agree steps along the way to make the changes easier for them.

Once you've done the time line a few times it will be in your head and you can conjure up the image and the steps without moving. This can be useful in situations when you can't actually move physically.

We can combine the time line with anchoring by firing our anchor at significant points along the line as triggers for change and to help us access a feeling of confidence in the future as we mentally time travel. This is particularly useful for grief.

How do we do it?

Imagine a line along the floor representing your life. Now stand at the point representing today, the present.

Step 1- Associate into it

What do you see in your life? What images come to the fore? Who do you see? If you are visual, give this colour, tone and form like a painting or a photograph.

What do you hear? Who can you hear? Is there music? What sounds do you hear? If you are auditory make these into a full orchestra of sound.

What do you feel? Are you warm or cold? Who is touching you? What are you doing? If you are kinaesthetic really move with the feeling.

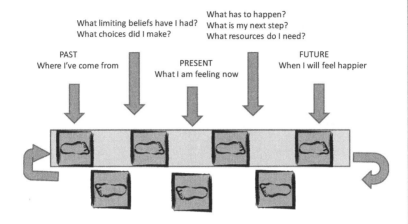

Step 2 – Move to where you want to be

This move will take you to a point on the line when you will feel happier, have achieved what you desire or have reached some significant point on your life's journey.

Associate into this point as you did in Step 1

Step 3 – Move back to the present

In order to get to the desired point things have to happen so what are the steps along the way to your goal? Walk through them one at a time, associating into each one.

Step 4 – Step back in time

Sometimes it can be helpful to step back along the time line if you find yourself saying 'I can't' or feel uncomfortable about something. By travelling back in time we can discover where these limiting beliefs came from and revisit them in terms of whether they serve us in our life now as a parent.

<u>For us</u>

Once we've had children we sometimes forget all the skills we had before and how useful they are to our parenting role.

By travelling back in time we can go to the point when we felt brave or had confidence, were able to negotiate, were good at rapport and so on.

Associate into those times in the past, anchor the skill and travel forward again back to the present and take them with you into your future.

<u>For our children</u>

You can travel back and forth along the time line and introduce it to your child.

For example if you are having problems getting them to eat vegetables introduce them to the time line, stand on today's point and ask them when they will eat vegetables.

Ask them to stand on that point saying 'yum yum' and fully associate into it.

Go back to the present and decide on what steps you can make towards that point.

You may be surprised to find the distance between today and when they will eat vegetables has already shortened.

5: CONFLICT

What is it?

In its broadest sense when we are not in rapport we are in conflict. This can be an internal conflict because we are out of kilter with our values or external conflict because we are not in rapport with those we are close to.

Sometimes the conflict is internal and we feel torn between two strong feelings inside us.

Here is a great exercise for internal conflict. It's called 'parts integration'.

Exercise

Hold out your right hand and imagine you are holding one of the values that you feel strongly about. Imagine the value, how you are manifesting it and all the aspects of it that are on your mind.

Now hold out the other hand and imagine you are holding the conflicting value or option. Again, build it up with all the aspects you have under consideration.

With both hands held outstretched in front of you, look at each of them in turn and imagine a small person on them representing that part of you. Ask person A (your right hand) what it wants for you, what is it's positive intent? Now do the same to person B on your left hand.

Are there common elements? Could the two 'people' agree a common goal and means of achieving it? Continue getting these two parts of you to offer solutions around the common positive goal until you feel you have a resolution.

Before you finish just check in with both parts that by agreeing there are no negative repercussions as a result of one part not doing what it wanted to do that will prove problematic.

External conflict, when you are not in rapport with your partner, someone at work or with your child can be very upsetting too. Read the worksheet on rapport to explore ways that you could improve your communication.

One way we can be in conflict is if there is a mismatch between the ways we each process and think.

Match/mismatch

Some people actively enjoy mismatching, disagreeing and looking for what is not OK. If you are a 'matcher' you will find this difficult so match the mismatching and copy the other person's language pattern and you will soon be in rapport.

Choices/Process

Do you enjoy choices or do you prefer to simply get on with the task. Someone who likes choices will find it difficult to make a decision so if you need them to, offer them a small range of choices about aspects that won't put you in conflict.

Towards/Away from

If you set goals and work towards them you will conflict with those whose goal is phrased negatively such as 'avoiding accidents' or 'avoiding work'. You will need to rephrase your words to match the way they process and thereby avoid conflict.

Associate/Disassociate

People who associate are excellent at showing empathy and understanding but lack the skills to separate the emotion from a situation and be analytical and solution focussed. Look it from the other person's point of view. The map is not the territory.

Big chunk/small chunk

Some like all the detail and are good at being thorough and others are good at seeing the big picture. Avoid conflict by matching the other person and seeing it from a different perspective.

You can 'chunk up' by asking 'what does this mean?' and 'chunk down' by asking 'how' questions to get to the detail.

By acknowledging that we all work differently and by matching and stepping into the other person's shoes we can achieve rapport.

What do we do though when even that has failed?

This is an exercise in perceptual positioning and it can be used very effectively to resolve conflict and enable you to see a situation from another person's point of view.

Exercise

Arrange three chairs in a triangle and sit in one. That is 'self' or 'first position'; the other chairs represent 'other' (the person you are not in rapport with) or 'second position' and 'spectator' who is an impartial witness or 'third position'.

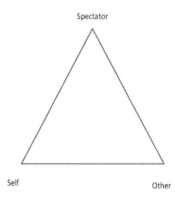

Express your feelings at this first position and then move to second position (other) and be that person. Imagine you are that person and express those views as if they were your own.

Return to first position and respond.

Move between the two chairs as if conducting a discussion until you and you as the other person have said all you want to say.

Now move to the third position and observe and comment on what has been said.

Return now to first position and say what you now feel and how you could achieve rapport.

You can introduce this to children as a great way to resolve sibling rivalry and they can put teddies or dolls on the chairs to remind them of who is who.

If your child has a problem at school with bullying this is a good way to help them understand the situation and give them the chance to practice being assertive in a safe environment.

AND FINALLY

If there is anything you are unsure about or would like to work on, please get in touch with me judy@engagingnlp.com or via my website www.engagingnlp.com and I would be happy to explain further or arrange an NLP coaching session.

References

NLP at work, Sue Knight, Nicholas Brealey Publishing

Happy Kids Happy You, Sue Beever, Crown House Publications

Brilliant Parent, Emma Sargent, Prentice Hall

The complete secrets of happy children, Steve & Sharon Thorsons, Biddulph

How to talk so kids will listen and listen so kids will talk Adele Faber & Elaine Mazlish, Simon & Schuster Audio

Teach yourself NLP, Steve Bavister & Amanda Vickers, Hodder

Bringing up happy children, Glenda Weil & Doro Marden, Hodder

The Satir Model, Virginia Satir, Science and Behavior Books

Think Good Feel Good, Paul Stallard, Wiley

Also from MX Publishing

Seeing Spells Achieving

The UK's leading NLP book for learning difficulties including dyslexia

Stop Bedwetting in 7 Days

A simple step-by-step guide to help children conquer bedwetting problems in just a few days

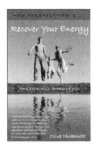

Recover Your Energy

NLP for Chronic Fatigue, ME and tiredness

More NLP books at www.mxpublishing.co.uk

Also from MX Publishing

Play Magic Golf

How to use self-hypnosis, meditation, Zen, universal laws, quantum energy, and the latest psychological and NLP techniques to be a better golfer

Psychobabble

A straight forward, plain English guide to the benefits of NLP

You Too Can Do Health

Improve Your Health and Wellbeing, Through the Inspiration of One Person's Journey of Self-development and Self-awareness Using NLP, energy and the Secret Law of Attraction

More NLP books at www.mxpublishing.co.uk

Also from MX Publishing

Process and Prosper

Inspiring and motivational book from necrotising faciitis survivor Wendy Harrington. Amazing book for anyone facing critical trauma.

Bangers and Mash

Battling throat cancer with the help of an NLP coach. Keith's story has led to changes in procedure in many cancer hospitals and is an inspiration to cancer patients everywhere.

Performance Strategies for Musicians

Tackle stage fright and performance anxiety using NLP.

More NLP books at www.mxpublishing.co.uk

Lightning Source UK Ltd.
Milton Keynes UK
UKOW06f0016141115

262680UK00001B/55/P

9 781907 685460